# 60 Organization That Will Give You Free Money

## (Grant)

## To Start a Business

## How To Access Free Money (Grant)?

Toyosi George Obayomi

ISBN: **9798843771393**

Cover design by: Art Painter

Library of Congress Control Number: 2018675309

Printed in the United States of America

This book is dedicated to the women in my life, my beloved mother

Mrs. Janet Olorunsola Arowosafe and my wife Mrs. Anuoluwapo Obayomi.

# Table of Contents

## Nugget 1: INTRODUCTION

The most common complaint among Nigerian youths attempting to start a business is a lack of capital. Many young people are unaware that several organizations have millions of dollars set aside for the funding of small businesses, non-governmental organizations, and small organizations.

These organizations include personal foundations, corporate CSR, government grants, and charitable organizations and other unique grants.

Some of the grants can be used to fund any type of business venture, while others cannot, and are intended to stimulate investment in specific sectors of the economy. For example, some grants are available for small businesses interested in green renewable energy or environmental conservation initiatives.

Some grants are also intended for non-profit organizations, women, and social enterprises.

In any case, every aspiring young entrepreneur should be aware of all available resources that would add qualitative value and empower all and sundry.

# Nugget 2: UNFPA SPECIAL YOUTH PROGRAMME GRANTS

This program is aimed to give young people from developing countries opportunities to engage in policy formation and programming; to help enhance the capacity of young people; and to sensitize both the young people and UNFPA personnel on partnering to solve adolescent and youth challenges.

**Grants/Financial Support:**

All selected candidates will be provided:

Cost of return travel from country of origin.

Assistance with travel documents and visa requirements.

Health insurance.

Housing arrangements.

Subsistence allowance (for meals and other basic needs).

A workstation and internet access.

Opportunities to be mentored by UNFPA staff on issues of interest.

Administrative assistance as required.

**Candidates should:**

Be between 20-24 years old during the fellowship.

be residents and nationals of a developing country (Applicants from developed countries will not be considered for this program, but are invited to apply for UNFPA's regular internship.

program).

have established interest and dedication to development issues through previous experiences or affiliation with a youth network or NGO working on development issues.

have basic leadership and advocacy skills.

have basic understanding of issues of importance to UNFPA and what the organization stands for.

have English language skills (written and oral).

have a commitment to return to home country to undertake follow up work with young

people.

**Website:** http://www.unfpa.org/

# Nugget 3: AGRI-VIE

Agri-Vie is a private equity investment fund focused on food and agribusiness in Sub-Sahara Africa. Since it started in 2008, it has invested over $100m in Africa's food and agribusiness sector.

Its investments in Africa include: Dew Crisp (South Africa), Africa Juice (Ethiopia), Fairfield Dairy (South Africa), New Forests Company (Tanzania), Hygrotech (South Africa), Kariki Group (Kenya)and Vida Oils (Mozambique). Entrepreneurs with viable projects in Nigeria and other African countries are free to apply.

Agri-Vie focuses on the following areas: food and beverages, convenience foods (including fresh-packed and prepared foods), protein products including poultry, aquaculture and beef; value-added dairy products, including yoghurts, desserts, cultured milk; health & wellness products; forestry and timber products; agricultural inputs including seeds, bio-friendly fertilizers and crop-protection; food logistics – cold chain, warehousing, distribution; and renewable energy.

**Contact information:**

Tel +27 (0)21 913 5662

Fax +27 (0)21 913 8954

E-Mail : office@agrivie.com

https://agrivie.com/

https://www.exeocapital.com/

The Access to Learning Award recognizes "creative groups that provide disadvantaged individuals with access to a world of online information."

The Global Libraries program of the foundation solicits applications from libraries and comparable institutions outside the United States that have developed innovative ways to provide these essential services:

Free public access to computers and the Internet; Public training to assist users in gaining access to online resources that can improve their lives; Technology training for library staff; and outreach to underserved populations.

Institutions from outside the United States that serve disadvantaged areas are eligible to apply. To be eligible, the applying institution must allow all members of the public to use computers and the Internet free of charge in a community space.

In addition, Bill & Melinda Gates Foundation looks for organizations that: Help reduce inequities in neglected areas Produce measurable results, catalyze increased momentum, scale, and sustainability of change Collaborate with government, philanthropic, private-sector, and not-for-profit partners.

Favor preventative approaches

Leverage support from other sources

Advance our current strategies, accelerating the work we are already supporting

The award recipient will receive $1 million.

**Contact:**

Bill & Melinda Gates Foundation, P.O Box 23350, Seattle, WA 98102.

**E-mail:** info@gatesfoundation.org

BBC World Challenge for Grassroots Projects: BBC World News and Newsweek, in partnership with Shell, have launched the World Challenge competition to uncover and honour grassroots projects and small enterprises from around the globe.

Annually, the World Challenge is held.

It is now soliciting nominations for creative projects or concepts that demonstrate an entrepreneurial spirit at work for the benefit of the community while taking a responsible stance.

The winner of the competition will earn a $20,000 award, while the runner-up and their finalist will each receive a $10,000 prize.

Winners may only utilize the grants for their own benefit and the advancement of their business. In addition, the winners will be invited to the ceremony when they will collect their prizes.

This ceremony will take place in the Netherlands and will be filmed and broadcast on BBC World News.

NB: This is a competition, and you must enter to have a chance of winning the grant.

Website: www.theworldchallenge.co.uk

# Nugget 6: BAMBOO FINANCE

Bamboo Finance is a commercial private equity firm specializing in investing in business models that benefit low-income communities in emerging markets. It has offices in Luxembourg, Geneva, Bogota, Nairobi and Singapore.

Launched in 2007, the firm seeks to demonstrate that private capital can be profitably deployed as a tool for effective change around the world. To date, Bamboo Finance manages about $250 million; representing two global funds and a combined portfolio of 46 investments operating in 30 emerging market countries. Investment focus Bamboo finance usually invests in businesses that satisfy the following conditions below:

The business must provide essential goods and/or services affordably to low-income communities unreached (or underserved) by existing businesses

The usage of its products/services should result in improvements in quality of life and/or efficiencies that translate into increased income or reduced expenses?

**Contact information:**

Email: info@bamboofinance.com

https://bamboocp.com/

+352 26 09 57

contact@bamboocp.com

compliance@bamboocp.com

# Nugget 7: AGRICULTURAL DEVELOPMENT GRANTS - BILL AND MELINDA GATES FOUNDATION

The mission of the Bill & Melinda Gates Foundation is to "enable people in developing nations to enjoy healthier and more productive lives."

The primary goals are to enhance people's health and provide them with the opportunity to pull themselves up and out of starvation and terrible poverty.

The foundation is working to end cycles of hunger and poverty by empowering small farmers in developing countries with the knowledge, resources, and opportunities they need to improve their production and earnings, as well as the quality of life they can provide for themselves and their families.

The goal of the Agricultural Development program of the Foundation is to assist subsistence farmers in developing nations in increasing their level of production and gaining access to relevant markets.

The following are the areas in which agricultural development funds are concentrated:

1. Enhanced productivity of agriculturalists: Efforts should be made to give less fortunate farmers access to more advanced inputs, as well as training and support networks, in order to assist those farmers in making more informed decisions, thereby enhancing their productivity and minimizing their impact on the environment.

2. Establishing links to markets - Seek to establish links for farmers to new and existing markets and give them access to information that will assist them in making decisions.

3. Emerging technologies - In the search for solutions that will be of assistance to small farmers, the partners apply a variety of strategies. These strategies vary from traditional seed breeding to the most recent biotechnologies.

4. Data, research, and policy analysis - This is accomplished through providing financial support for the collecting of data, the conduct of research related to agricultural development, and the study of policies pertaining to agricultural development. This is absolutely necessary for determining the efficacy of the many ways that have been taken, for providing small farmers with correct information, and for determining the implications of national and international agricultural policy. For more information, visit: Agricultural Development Grants - Bill and Melinda Gates Foundation.

https://www.gatesfoundation.org/our-work/programs/global-growth-and-opportunity/agricultural-development

- Phone: (206) 709-3400
- Email: media@gatesfoundation.org

# Nugget 8: THE BANK OF INDUSTRY GRADUATE ENTERPRENUSHIP FUND (GEF)

Launched on October 5, 2015, the Graduate Entrepreneurship Fund (GEF) is a special empowerment initiative designed specifically for active members of the National Youth Service Corps (NYSC). The program has a total allocation of N2.0 billion. The Bank of Industry (BOI) and the National Youth Service Corps (NYSC) have come up with an innovative plan that aims to accomplish the following things, and it is a collaborative venture between the two organizations:

- Encourage graduates of tertiary institutions currently undergoing the compulsory one-year NYSC program, to venture into business and become employers of labour rather than job seekers.
- Address the entrepreneurship capacity gap of the NYSC members who are expected to produce bankable business plans after the three-day capacity building program.
- Deepen financial inclusion by de-risking the NYSC members and making them eligible for concessional loans ranging between N500,000 and N2 million to be provided by BOI.
- Ensure sustainability of the businesses of the eventual loan beneficiaries through effective monitoring by the NYSC Directorate and BOI.

Website: http://www.boi.ng/aboutgef/

# Nugget 9: ACUMEN FUND

The Rockefeller Foundation, the Cisco Systems Foundation, and three other private philanthropists provided the initial funding for the charitable organization Acumen when it was established in 2001. The Acumen Fund makes investments in individuals who have the potential to bring about the development of sustainable solutions to significant issues.

The Acumen Fund made a joint investment of $1.5 million in Esoko Networks Limited ("Esoko") in May of 2014. Esoko is a technology platform that was developed in Ghana and connects African farmers to markets through the use of mobile phones. In October of 2014, Acumen made public their decision to invest $1.4 million in SolarNow, a firm that markets and provides financing for residential solar energy systems in Uganda.

The nonprofit organisation Acumen is always looking for business people with novel and creative ideas for combating poverty who also satisfy the organization's criteria for investment. In order to be eligible for investment, business owners must have their primary location in East Africa, West Africa, India, Pakistan, or Latin America, as well as significant operations or impacts in those regions.

**Contact Information:**

+233 030 298 4098 (West Africa)

+254 736 073036 (East Africa)

https://acumenacademy.org/


# Nugget 10: AFRICA PRIZE FOR ENGINEERING INNOVATION

Countries within sub-Saharan Africa are considered eligible for participation in this program. For the purposes of the competition, the following countries are considered to be part of the sub-Saharan region: Angola, Benin, Botswana, Burkina Faso, Burundi, Cameroon, Cape Verde, Central African Republic, Chad, Comoros, Republic of the Congo, Democratic Republic of the Congo, Côte d'Ivoire, Djibouti, Equatorial Guinea, Eritrea, Ethiopia, Gabon, The Gambia

To be completed in (country): the countries of sub-Saharan Africa

A concise summary of the Africa Prize for Engineering Innovation is as follows: the competition is available to aspirational and talented engineers from sub-Saharan Africa who work in any engineering field and can display innovative and entrepreneurial engineering talents.

**Eligible Field of Study:** Any engineering field

**About the Prize:**

- The objective of the Africa Prize for Engineering Innovation is to encourage and recognize entrepreneurial endeavors in the field of engineering in sub-Saharan Africa. The Africa Prize will inspire ambitious and talented engineers from sub-Saharan Africa to apply their abilities to discover solutions to local difficulties that can be scaled up. This will highlight the relevance of engineering as a driver of improved quality of life and economic growth.
- Through a period of six months of training and mentoring, a shortlist of inventive applicants will get essential financial support for commercialization of their ideas. After this period of mentorship, the finalists will be invited to present at an event that will be held in Africa, and a winner will be chosen to receive a prize of £25,000, along with runners-up who will each receive a prize of £10,000.
- Qualifications Required to Apply: Applicants must be individuals or groups of no more than three people.

- Individual applicants must be citizens of a country within sub-Saharan Africa and currently reside there. For teams of two or three, the lead applicant must be a citizen of a country within sub-Saharan Africa and currently reside there.
- Applicants must have an engineering innovation and provide a letter of support from a university of research institution.

- Industrial researchers and establishments are not eligible.
- The applicant's innovation can be any new product, technology or service, based on research in engineering defined in its broadest sense to encompass a wide range of fields, including: agricultural technology, biotechnology, chemical engineering, civil engineering, computer science, design engineering, electrical and electronic engineering, ICT, materials science, mechanical engineering, and medical engineering. If you are in any doubt that your area of expertise would be considered engineering then please contact the Academy to discuss your application.
- Applicants should have achieved the development of, and be in the early stages of commercializing, an engineering innovation that:

1. will bring social and/or environmental benefits to country/countries in sub-Saharan

Africa;

2. has strong potential to be replicated and scaled up;

3. is accompanied by an ambitious but realistic business plan which has strong commercial viability.

**Number of Awardees:** Not specified

Value of Prize: Finalists will be invited to present at an event held in Africa and a winner will be selected to receive £25,000 along with runners-up, who will each be awarded £10,000

**Duration of Program:** Crucial commercialization support is awarded to a shortlist of innovative applicants, through a six-month period of training and mentoring.

To apply, visit

## Nugget 11: AMERICAN JEWISH WORLD SERVICE - AJWS

The American Jewish Globe Service (AJWS) is a worldwide development organization that serves people of all different races, religions, and nationalities in order to alleviate the effects of poverty, hunger, and sickness in those regions of the world that are still developing. The American Jewish World Service (AJWS) awards grants ranging from $3,000 to $30,000 each year; however, preference is given to grants submitted by smaller groups with annual budgets of less than $300,000.

The grants are typically given out for a period of one year at a time, with the option to renew them annually.

Only the following countries in Africa get funding from the American Jewish World Service (AJWS): Chad, Democratic Republic of Congo, Ethiopia, Ghana, Kenya, Liberia, Nigeria, Rwanda, Senegal, Somalia, South Africa, Sudan, Uganda, Zambia, and Zimbabwe. The American Jewish World Service funds non-governmental (NGOs) and community-based

organizations in Africa working in the following thematic areas:

## 1. Sustainable Livelihoods and Sustainable Development:

These includes:

Sustainable Agriculture and Biodiversity.

Food Security.

Land and Resource Rights.

Economic Opportunities.

Slum and Urban Development

## 2. Community Health:

These includes:

HIV/AIDS care and support.

Anti-stigma efforts, and advocacy.

Disease prevention and control through health education and nutrition with a focus on

HIV/AIDS

TB and Malaria

Reproductive Health and Rights.

Maternal and Child Health and Rights.

Efforts to strengthen community and government health systems.

Violence Prevention.

## 3. Education for All:

Facilitating access to quality primary and secondary education for all. This includes:

Access to government and non-formal education with a focus on retention for girls and orphans and vulnerable children.

Improving the quality of education, including teacher training, curriculum development and fostering community engagement and oversight of schools.

Vocational and literacy training for youth and adults Early Childhood Development.

## 4. Community Engagement in Conflict and Emergencies:

Supporting local organizations affected by disasters and conflict to move to move toward peace and development.

## 5. Community Voice: Civic and Political Participation:

AJWS funds policy advocacy and community mobilization efforts that are led by community-based organizations working for:

Women's Rights

Indigenous Rights

Religious and Ethnic Minority Rights

Sexual Minority Rights

Refugee and Internally Displaced Persons Rights

Worker Rights

Youth and Adolescent Participation **AJWS does not fund:**

Proselytizing activities.

Individuals.

Orphanages.

Political parties.

Hospitals.

Private enterprises.

Government structures.

Letters of inquiry are accepted throughout the year.

Website: www.ajws.org

45 West 36th Street

New York, NY 10018

- 212.792.2900

- 800.889.7146

- 212.792.2930

- ajws@ajws.org

# Nugget 12: USAID DEVELOPMENT GRANTS PROGRAM

Development Grants Program of the United States Agency for International Development (USAID): The United States Agency for International Development (USAID), through the Office of Innovation and Development Alliances (IDEA), Local Sustainability (LS) Division, is inviting applications for grants under the Development Grants Program from local non-governmental organizations (LNGOs) as well as private and voluntary organizations in the United States.

Through innovation (which refers to advances in development impact that are major rather than incremental) and partnership, the IDEA Office aims to achieve development goals more swiftly, cost-efficiently, sustainably, and at a wider scale. The Local Support Division of the IDEA organization works toward the goal of enhancing the long-term viability of civil society groups by concentrating its efforts on the promotion of creative local development projects and the enhancement of capacity.

The overall goal of the DGP is to contribute to improved and sustainable grass-roots development by supporting development projects and strengthening the capacities of nascent development partners in countries where the DGP is active. This will be accomplished through the DGP's involvement in the following countries: In recognition of the fact that a vibrant and active NGO sector is fundamental to the promotion of a healthy democracy that is accountable and responsive to the needs of citizens, the DGP has made the strengthening of local nongovernmental organizations and public voluntary organizations in the United States a priority.

Nongovernmental organizations (NGOs) in certain countries may be eligible to submit applications for certain sectors. These sectors may include, but are not limited to: rural development; basic education; microenterprise; health (HIV/AIDS); water; democracy and governance; business advocacy; energy efficiency awareness; and so on.

Website: https://www.usaid.gov/partnership-opportunities/ngo/development-grants-program

We collaborate with organizations all around the world to provide
financial support for a diverse range of pioneering educational
initiatives in indigenous communities. We are able to assist in providing
people with the opportunity to experience life to its fullest by expanding

their access to information and learning opportunities. Feed the Minds is a nonprofit organization that provides financial support to separate initiatives with the objective of improving the quality of life in underserved communities through the promotion of literacy, open lines of communication, and access to relevant information.

Grants from Feed the Minds can range anywhere from £1,000 to £25,000 in value. During the past two years, we have provided financial assistance to projects located in over thirty different nations across the continents of Africa, Asia, South America, and the Eastern Block. Applications for financing can be filed for a period of up to three years, and the total amount awarded to each project cannot exceed $25,000.

We want all applications to highlight the engagement of local people in the project design and implementation since Feed the Minds places a strong emphasis on the importance of establishing indigenous remedies to issues. Feed the Minds provides funding for education across the entire developmental spectrum, as well as teaching that is culturally relevant and conducted in the native tongues of the students. Additionally, the indigenous creative process as well as publications geared for the local community are emphasized by Feed the Minds.

The funding for training that is provided by Feed the Minds is ecumenical, and we welcome suggestions from all different denominations. Feed the Minds will not provide financial support to organizations or initiatives that practice discrimination against individuals on the basis of their religion, gender, colour, disability, or sexual orientation.

Feed the Minds does not provide financial support to projects that promote loyalty to particular political parties or regimes. In addition, we do not provide funding for projects involving capital expenditures, tuition fees, or research.

Website: http://www.feedtheminds.org/

# Nugget 14: CAPTAIN PLANET FOUNDATION GRANTS

The Captain Planet Foundation's objective is to provide financial assistance and support for children and young people's environmental projects that involve direct participation. The mission of the Foundation is to foster creative programming that equips children and young people all over the world to tackle environmental issues in their own communities and neighborhoods, both on an individual and a group level, and to do so through collaborative efforts.

The Foundation is of the opinion that children can develop a greater understanding and appreciation for the world in which they live by participating in environmental education programs.

**Grant Guidelines:**

In order to be considered for funding, proposals must:

Promote understanding of environmental issues

Focus on hands-on involvement

Involve children and young adults 6-18

Promote interaction and cooperation within the group

Help young people develop planning and problem-solving skills

Include adult supervision

Commit to follow-up communication with the Foundation (specific requirements are

explained once the grant has been awarded)

Grant Proposals are reviewed over a period of three months from the date of the submission deadline.

Website: http://www.captainplanetfoundation.org/

Nugget 15: COMMONWEALTH YOUTH AWARDS

Investment in youth-led development is encouraged and maintained thanks to the Commonwealth Youth Awards. The awards bring attention to the role that young people play in the accomplishment of development goals.

Youth workers are encouraged to submit young people who are leading innovative programs in any number of fields, including agriculture, small enterprise, skills training, climate change/environmental protection, sustainable livelihoods, and poverty reduction. Some examples of these sectors include: The Commonwealth Youth Program (CYP), which is responsible for promoting the awards, does so in an effort to increase the profile of young people who are integrally involved in the process of change and who are working side by side with decision-makers for a more secure future and to highlight the contribution that these young people have made.

The young men and women who are chosen to get prizes also receive recognition on a national, as well as a regional and worldwide level. Through its four regional centers in Africa, Asia, the Caribbean, and the Pacific, CYP collaborates with the fifty-four countries that make up the Commonwealth of Nations.

There will be four finalists from each region of the Commonwealth, with the best entry from each region receiving an award for being the winner of that region, and the winner of the best regional award winning the award for the entire Commonwealth. Winners receive money to further the work of their projects, and they are also required to maintain close communication with the CYP regarding the most effective method to put the funding to use.

Candidates for the prizes must fall within the age range of 15 to 29 years old.

Evans Wadongo, a native of Kenya, was recently honoured with the Commonwealth Youth Award for both the entire Commonwealth and the Africa area. He was awarded a grant in the amount of £5,000 for the charity that he had established, which is called "Use solar, save lives." A prize of £3,000 was awarded to each of the regional winners in Asia, the Caribbean, and the Pacific.

Mr. Wadongo came up with the idea for a solar-powered light that used recycled materials when he was 19 years old. Over 27,000 of these lanterns have been manufactured and distributed all over the country of

Kenya. They offer an alternate lighting option to kerosene lamps that is safer, less expensive, and friendlier to the environment. His concept has been expanded to include the construction of regional youth centers, which will offer young people with opportunities to develop their abilities.

Website: http://thecommonwealth.org/

## Nugget 16: EDUCATING AFRICA AWARDS FOR ENTREPRENEURSHIP IN EDUCATION

Teach A Man To Fish was the group that came up with the idea for the competition known as the Educating Africa Awards for Entrepreneurship in Education, which is generously supported by Educating Africa, one of Teach A Man To Fish's partner organizations. It continues to recognize and reward organizations in Africa that make use of novel and entrepreneurial approaches to close the educational service gaps that exist across the continent.

The competition is open to any and all organizations headquartered in

Africa that engage in the field of education, including primary, secondary, and university education, in addition to adult education and non-formal education. In addition to a first prize of $10,000, two runner-up prizes of $5,000 each, and fifty awards of $1,000 each for the best entry from each country on the continent, the competition has a total prize pool of $30,000.

**Entrepreneurship in Education Awards:**

TeachAManToFish are looking for the very best programs and models for education.

They're entrepreneurial.

They're sustainable.

They create impact.

**Entry Criteria:**

Entry is open to all organizations actively carrying out education work in Africa – however preference will be given to those which have been in existence more than two years, are legally registered, and which maintain good financial records of their activities.

For an institution to be eligible it must be based in one of the 54 African countries for which prizes are available.

Entrants must supply the work contact details of a suitable referee who can confirm that

their entry is true and accurate.

Referees must be independent of your organization and or a government official, qualified

professional, or internationally recognized institution.

Education Awards Entry Details

Entrants will be required to briefly describe the background to their program and its success in

rising to the challenges of education in Africa.

Website: http://www.teachamantofish.org.uk/pan-african-awards

# Nugget 17: AFRICAN WOMEN'S DEVELOPMENT FUND (AWDF)

The African Women's Development Fund (AWDF) is the continent's first pan-African women's grant maker. Since the beginning of its activities in 2001, the African Women's Development Fund (AWDF) has distributed grants totaling US$17 million to 800 women's organizations located in 42 different African countries. The African Women's Development Fund (AWDF) is a fund that intends to assist foster a culture of learning and collaborations within the African women's movement. This fund is an institutional capacity-building and program development fund. In addition to providing financial support and grants, the African Women's

Development Fund (AWDF) will work to improve the organizational capacities of the groups that receive funding from it.

Women's Human Rights; Economic Empowerment and Livelihoods; Governance, Peace and Security; Reproductive Health and Rights; HIV/AIDS; Arts, Culture, and Sports; AWDF Only Funds Local, National, Sub-Regional, and Regional Organizations in Africa Working Towards Empowering Women Women's Human Rights; Economic Empowerment and Livelihoods; Governance, Peace and Security; Reproductive Health and Rights; HIV/AIDS; Arts, Culture, and Sports; The AWDF does not give funds to individuals but rather exclusively to organizations. It gives out grants with amounts ranging from $8,000 all the way up to $50,000.

**Contact Information:**

Office: Plot 78 Ambassadorial Enclave, East Legon, Ghana

Email: AWDF@awdf.org or grants@awdf.org

https://awdf.org/

Tel: + 233 302 521257 Fax: +233 302 521257

# Nugget 18: WORLD FOOD PRIZE

The Food Prize is a monetary prize of two hundred and fifty thousand dollars that is given out publicly at the Laureate Award Ceremony in the middle of October, on or around World Food Day. This ceremony takes place in conjunction with the Borlaug Dialogue international symposium. This award will recognize an individual under the age of 40 who has clearly demonstrated intellectual courage, stamina, and determination in the fight to eliminate global hunger and poverty. The recipient of this award will be selected based on their exceptional, science-based achievement in international agriculture and food production.

This award will be given to a person who is working closely and directly "in the field" or at the production or processing level with farmers, animal herders, fishers, or others who live and work in rural communities, in any field or enterprise that spans the entire food production, processing, and distribution chain. The award will be given to a person who is working closely and directly "in the field" or at the production or processing level with farmers.

**World Food Prize Eligibility & Criteria:**

- Nominees must be under the age of 40
- Nominees must be actively working in the discipline, research area, position, or on the project(s) for which they are being recognized. They may be associated with a public or private educational, research or development organization or related entity.
- Nominees remain eligible for consideration beyond the year of their nomination, at the discretion of the Award Jury, as long as the award criteria and age requirement are met.
- The award is intended to be presented to one person. In unusual and rare circumstances, another person may share the award for pronounced collaborative efforts and achievement.
- World Food Prize - Documents Required
- All nominations must be submitted in English online.
- A concise statement (3000-word limit) explaining and describing-

1. The nominee's work and accomplishments, with details and examples that illustrate several of the criteria specified for this award

2. How, in doing this work, the nominee reflects the attributes demonstrated by Dr. Borlaug during his early career

3. The impact or results of the nominee's work.

- Nominee's Curriculum Vitae or resume, including date of birth, country of origin,
  education, and professional background.
- One (1) nomination letter and two (2) letters of support describing, explaining and
  emphasizing the main achievements of the nominee must be provided with the nomination. Due to the high volume of nominations, please do not submit more than two support letters.
- Photos: A head shot of the nominee is required (minimum 300 dpi resolution); 2 additional action photos of the nominee at work may also be submitted.

Website: www.worldfoodprize.org

# Nugget 19: GEF SMALL GRANTS

The United Nations Development Program (UNDP), on behalf of the Global Environment Facility (GEF) partnership, and the United Nations Office for Project Services (UNOPS) are responsible for the implementation, management, and oversight of the Small Grants program (SGP), which receives funding as a corporate program from the Global Environment Facility (GEF) (UNOPS).

To this day, the Global Environment Facility has contributed around $401 million to the program's budget. In addition, the program has received monetary and in-kind contributions amounting to a total of $407 million from a variety of different partners. Supporting communities in their efforts to achieve more sustainable livelihoods is not only possible, but extremely important in bringing about change and achieving global environmental benefits. This has been successfully demonstrated by the Small Grants Program, which has been working with communities around the world to combat the most critical environmental problems for nearly two decades. The program has been working with communities to combat the most critical environmental problems for nearly two decades.

SGP has a presence in 122 countries and has awarded more than 12,000 grants all over the world. It provides financial assistance to non-governmental and community-based organizations in developing countries so that they can carry out projects that demonstrate how community action can preserve the delicate balance that exists between human needs and environmental imperatives.

The reduction and adaptation to the effects of climate change, the preservation of biological diversity, the safeguarding of international waters, the mitigation of the harmful effects of persistent organic pollutants, and the protection of land from degradation are the primary focuses of the program.

The SGP will consider funding requests for the following kind of activities, among others:

Community-based needs analysis and planning (funding for future planning): There are limited grant monies available, often not exceeding $2,000 USD, that can be used to assist pre-project participatory assessment and planning activities. These activities are intended to strengthen community participation in the identification and implementation of projects.

Pilot demonstration activities: The majority of initiatives that receive funding are endeavours that investigate and demonstrate the practicability of novel community-based solutions to global environmental issues. Although the majority of demonstration projects include capacity development components, grants may be awarded for targeted technical assistance and training activities that focus on developing CBO and NGO capacities in the GEF's focal areas. These activities focus on developing CBO and NGO capacities in the GEF's focal areas.

Monitoring and analysis: Grants funds may also be made available to intermediary non-governmental organizations (NGOs) and research centers (including universities) in order to support program monitoring; to assist in identifying, assessing, and documenting best practices; and to prepare case studies of SGP-supported projects. It is also advised that monitoring and analysis operations make use of methodologies that involve participant input. Discussions on policy, networking, and information sharing: There are grant funds available to support the dissemination of innovations and best practices, relevant networking activities, and policy dialogue efforts that are aimed at promoting a policy environment that is supportive of community-level action in the GEF focal areas. This is done in order to leverage the experience gained from SGP project work.

https://sgp.undp.org/

304 East 45th Street, 9th Floor

New York, NY, 10017

Phone: +1 646 781 4385

Email: sgp.info@undp.org

This competition is a group effort with the goal of locating and showcasing innovators, both individuals and organizations, that directly or indirectly promote tourism in a way that maintains or improves the geographical character of a place, as well as its environment, culture, aesthetics, heritage, and the quality of life for the people who live there.

The competition is accessible to all types of organizations from all nations, including charitable organizations, private organizations, and public organizations. All submissions are required to explain how a particular program or activity is novel and distinctive. The projects must be further along than just an idea, and they must be able to demonstrate their success on a local, regional, or global scale.

The innovation needs to demonstrate that it has the ability to become self-sustaining and to be successfully copied in other locations.

A cash prize in the amount of $5,000 will be awarded to each of the three winners. Both English and Spanish are acceptable for entry submissions.

Link: https://www.changemakers.com/geotourism-challenge-celebrating-places-changing-lives

## Nugget 21: CDC

CDC is the Development Finance Institution (DFI) of the United Kingdom and was established in 1948. It is completely owned by the Department for International Development of the United Kingdom Government (DFID). It is the oldest development finance institution in the world and has a track record of making profitable investments in companies that have gone on to become market leaders.

The CDC provides active support to firms located throughout Africa and South Asia, and the total value of its portfolio of assets exceeds £2.5 billion (year end 2013). Feronia is an agricultural production and processing enterprise concentrating on palm oil plantations and arable farming in the Democratic Republic of the Congo. In November of 2013, the CDC made the announcement that they will be investing $18.1 million in Feronia (DRC).

Website: www.cdcgroup.com

## Nugget 22: IsDB BUSINESS PLAN COMPETITION

Regarding the Countries of Sub-Saharan Africa. The Islamic Development Bank Business Plan Competition is a relatively new project that was recently launched by the IsDB Group. Candidates participate in this competition in order to build and further refine their business ideas in preparation for the launch of their start-ups or the expansion of their operations, all while competing for cash awards! As of the year 2014, the competition offered cash awards ($25,000 for the winner of the first place, $15,000 for the winner of the second place, and $10,000 for the winner of the third place in each track of the competition), mentorship, and networking opportunities.

Follow this link: https://www.isdb.org/

**Address:**

8111 King Khalid St.

Al Nuzlah Al Yamania Dist. Unit No. 1

Jeddah 22332-2444

Kingdom of Saudi Arabia

**Phone:** KSA Phone: +966 12 6361400

**Fax:** +966 126366871

**Email:** info@isdb.org

# Nugget 23: UNITED STATES AFRICAN DEVELOPMENT FOUNDATION

The African Development Foundation (ADF) is an independent federal agency within the United States government that was established to support African-led development that grows community enterprises by providing seed capital and technical support. The mission of the African

Development Foundation (ADF) is to help grow community businesses in Africa. USADF facilitates the connection of community businesses with financial resources and technical assistance. It provides assistance to organizations and businesses in Africa, making it easier for them to generate and maintain employment opportunities, increase their levels of income, increase their level of food security, and address the requirements of human development.

Only in 2014, the United States African Development Foundation distributed 336 grants totaling more than $50 million, positively affecting the lives of over 1.3 million people in Africa. The United States Army Dependents' Fund focuses its attention on recovering communities, young people, women and girls, and small-holder farmers. It gives grants of up to two hundred and fifty thousand dollars directly to community organizations that are either too difficult to reach or underserved and are prepared to do their part.

## Contact Information:

1400 Street NW, Suite 1000,

Washington. D.C. 20005-2248, USA

P: 202-673-3916 | Tel: 202.673.3810

Tel: +254 20 269 9137/8/9

Email: info@adf.gov

https://www.usadf.gov/apply

Shiffon has begun a competition for aspiring female entrepreneurs in order to find solutions to the problems that women confront. The winners of the competition will be given the opportunity to begin initiatives in their home countries.

Concerning the Award: Women's participation in the labour force is directly proportional to the rate of economic growth. Shiffon is a luxury jewellery design enterprise that combines business and social purpose with the goal of breaking this cycle and empowering women and girls all over the world. In many parts of the world, women have limited access to the opportunities and financial resources necessary to build a life of their own.

Two students at Harvard University came together to start Shiffon with the intention of creating a society in which women and girls from all over the world have the freedom to pursue possibilities that have no limits. Shiffon is an ethically sourced company that donates fifty percent of its profits to organizations that support the advancement of women. Social responsibility is ingrained in every facet of the company's operations. The United Nations Women and the Startup Girl foundation are two of the organizations that Shiffon works closely with as active partners.

Type: Entrepreneurship, Contest

**Eligibility:**

- The competition is open to budding entrepreneurs passionate about launching enterprises that are driven to empower women and provide employment opportunities.
- Applications are open to those who are in the ideation/early stages of a social venture, or are launching a new subsidiary or offshoot of an existing social enterprise.
- Submissions are not only limited to women; men with initiatives whose purpose is to support women's empowerment is welcome to apply.

**Number of Awardees:** 5

**Benefits of the Program:** Shiffon will provide successful applicants with the opportunity to win one of five prizes totaling $5,000 and receive mentoring from prominent fashion and technology companies and consultancies. They are aware that providing fledgling companies with mentorship in addition to financial support is essential to the companies' growth and development.

To apply, visit: https://www.oneyoungworld.com/

info@oneyoungworld.com

## Nugget 25: WORLD INNOVATION SUMMIT FOR EDUCATION AWARDS

Awards presented by the World Innovation Summit for Education (WISE) Applications for the WISE Awards are now being accepted by the World Innovation Summit for Education (WISE). The awards recognize, exhibit, and promote each year six innovative educational initiatives that are having a revolutionary influence on society and education. Each year, the projects are selected from a pool of applicants.

Each winning initiative will earn $20,000 in prize money in addition to exposure on a global scale (US). In addition to this, the projects that win the WISE Awards and those that are finalists receive support and visibility through WISE media and communication channels such as film productions, participation in the annual WISE Summit and collaborative events where the projects are presented on a global stage, and the publication of WISE Books.

These educational models are brought to light by WISE in order to highlight the beneficial impact they may make to a community or society as well as their potential for scalability. WISE is cultivating a community of educational pioneers one year at a time, creating an atmosphere that is ideal for the formation of ground-breaking partnerships.

Depending on the circumstances, innovations might take the form of a wide variety of various things. As a result, the goal of WISE is to shed light on the most cutting-edge ideas and solutions now available to the educational problems that are plaguing the whole world. Applications can be submitted by project holders located in any location, educational sector, or level as long as they demonstrate the quality and effect of their activities in compliance with the requirements.

WISE encourages anybody who is working in a project that improves access to excellent education, develops innovative educational technology and methodologies, or offers new opportunities for lifelong learning to submit an application for the Awards.

https://www.wise-qatar.org/wise-works/wise-awards/

The Nansen Refugee Award is the highest honour that can be bestowed upon a person or organization by the United Nations High Commissioner for Refugees (UNHCR). It is presented annually to a person or organization "in recognition of extraordinary and dedicated service to refugees." It is open to participation by any individual or group based in any nation, regardless of creed, colour, age, or profession.

Anyone can submit a nomination for an individual or organization to be considered for the Award. The UN High Commissioner for Refugees (UNHCR) has established a special committee to choose the ultimate winner. The Award consists of a commemorative medal and a monetary reward of one hundred thousand dollars in United States currency, both of which were generously presented by the governments of Norway and Switzerland. The recipient of the Nansen Award will receive a monetary prize in addition to the award, and the purpose of this prize is to "enable the recipient to pursue refugee assistance projects drawn up in consultation with UNHCR." "The recipient of the Nansen Award will be given a monetary prize in addition to the award, and the purpose of this prize is to enable the recipient to pursue refugee assistance projects that have been developed in consultation with UNHCR. To this day, refugees in countries such as Cambodia, Botswana, and Venezuela have benefited from programs that are part of the so-called Nansen Fund."

Nominations can be filed through the UNHCR website, which is accessible online.

Website: http://www.unhcr.org/nansen-refugee-award.html

## Nugget 27: Google RISE Awards

The RISE initiative supports and links not-for-profit groups throughout the world to enhance equality in Computer Science education with an emphasis on girls, minorities who are traditionally underrepresented in the discipline, and youngsters from low-income neighbourhoods.

Google thinks that technology will continue to play an essential role in defining our future, and the young of today will help invent and drive these technologies for years to come. We hope that all children will one day have the chance to develop their potential and achieve great things in science. To that end, we strive to help students come one step closer to reaching their potential by giving organizational growth and development opportunities through the Google RISE Awards.

**RISE Awards include:**

- Capacity Building: Access to a 12-month capacity program that exposes candidates to Google expertise.
- Financial: Grants of $10,000 – $25,000
- Operational Support: Customized to the needs of the organization such as volunteers or pro-bono consulting
- A community of Practice: Continued peer engagement through a community of practice connects awardees, alumni, and beyond so that communities around the world can learn from best practices and lessons learned.
- Fields of Interest: Science, Technology, Engineering, and Mathematics (STEM), as well as Computer Science (CS)
- Who is Eligible? Organizations from around the globe who are working to promote and support Science, Technology, Engineering, and Mathematics (STEM), as well as Computer Science (CS). with emphasis on increasing engagement of socioeconomically disadvantaged students, girls, and under-represented minorities are eligible for consideration.

**Program Guidelines:**

- Google RISE Awards are specifically geared towards STEM and CS educational and outreach programs around the world
- Applications are encouraged from organizations and educational institutions regardless of the socio-economic status, race, or gender of the students they serve
- Please note that the RISE team is not able to provide one on one consultations during the review process (both prior to applying

and after applications have been submitted) to ensure no bias is given to specific organizations.

If you have additional questions about whether or not your organization meets these eligibility requirements, please contact: google-rise@google.com

https://edu.google.com/code-with-google/

# Nugget 28: ALLIANCE FOR A GREEN REVOLUTION IN AFRICA (AGRA)

The Alliance for a Green Revolution in Africa (AGRA) is a partnership between The Rockefeller Foundation and The Bill and Melinda Gates Foundation that works with African governments, other donors, non-governmental organizations (NGOs), the private sector, and African farmers to significantly and sustainably improve the levels of productivity and income enjoyed by low-income, small-scale farmers in Africa.

AGRA's primary operations include policy advocacy and the collection of resources. The organization's headquarters are located in Nairobi, Kenya, and it also has a branch office in Accra, Ghana. AGRA's Program for Africa's Seeds Systems (PASS) is an initiative that aims to improve food security and reduce poverty in Africa. This will be accomplished by promoting the development of seed delivery systems that will enable small-scale farmers to obtain access to improved and adapted crop varieties in a manner that is equitable and sustainable.

AGRA is looking for duly qualified organizations to submit proposals for funding of up to $150,000 over the course of two years for activities that will allow the grantee to improve the production and distribution of certified seed of improved, adapted crop varieties among poor, small-scale farmers through both private and public channels, such as seed companies, community-based seed systems, and public research and extension services. AGRA will select one grantee to receive the funding.

Activities that raise farmer knowledge of the value of enhanced seed and expand seed distribution channels through agro dealers and other seed merchants should be included in any proposals that are submitted in this area. Proposals that center on the production and distribution of large quantities of high-quality seed of a diverse range of crop species to low-income, small-scale farmers at the most affordable price will be given priority. AGRA Call for Proposals - Eligible countries include Ethiopia, Kenya, Uganda, Tanzania, Rwanda,

Malawi, Zambia, Mozambique, Ghana, Nigeria, Mali, Niger and Burkina Faso.

**Contact:**

**Website:** www.agra.org/grants

**Head Office:**

Alliance for a Green Revolution in Africa (AGRA)

West End Towers, 4th Floor

Kanjata Road, off Muthangari Drive, Off Waiyaki Way

P.O. Box 66773

Westlands 00800

Tel: +254 (20) 3675 000 / +254 (703) 033 000

USA : +1 650 833 7010

# Nugget 29: TOTAL STARTUPPER OF THE YEAR AWARD

In Africa, like in other parts of the world, a lot of young people have the dream of starting their own company and creating a better future for themselves. Because of this, Total came up with the idea for the Start upper of the year challenge. You are qualified to participate in this competition if you are in the process of formulating a business plan or if you are in the preliminary stages of establishing your own company. Each winner will receive individualized business coaching to assist him or her in starting a business or further developing an existing one. The winner will get financial support of up to $30,000 (in their respective native currencies) from Total.

Follow this link to apply:

## Nugget 30: HULT PRIZE STUDENT ENTERPRISE CHALLENGE

With the seventh annual Hult Prize, thousands of university students from across the world will collaborate to establish start-ups that will address a problem that affects billions of people. Over 10,000 applications will begin the trip, and only 300 start-ups from across the world will be selected to pitch their business ideas in one of five global locations: Boston, San Francisco, London, Dubai, and Shanghai. A $1,000,000 grand prize will be given in Washington, D.C.

Concerning the Award: The Hult Prize Foundation is a start-up accelerator for aspiring young social entrepreneurs from throughout the world. The annual Hult Prize competition, named one of the top five ideas transforming the world by President Bill Clinton and TIME Magazine, strives to produce and launch the most appealing social business concepts—start-up firms that address serious challenges confronting billions of people. The winners will get a USD1 million seed capital prize, as well as mentorship and assistance from the worldwide business community.

1. The Hult Prize Foundation estimates the overall number of worldwide refugees to be one billion, rather than the UN-accepted figure of 60 million.

2. The refugee cycle has been restructured into four stages: pre-movement, in-movement, temporary relocation, and permanent status.

3. The 2017 Challenge identifies extremely specific areas for disruptive innovation at each stage of the cycle.

4. Refugees represent one of the most significant untapped economic possibilities in the world.

5. Reawakening human potential in refugees on the move reveals the need for social innovation in a variety of social service categories.

This case study will serve as your blueprint for developing your social enterprise. It will be available in early October. It was developed specifically for this year's Hult Prize and takes a deep dive into the path of a refugee, beginning when movement becomes a possibility - not a reality. Where previous organizations have failed, we believe the Hult Prize may succeed by challenging young people throughout the world to reinvent how to convert one of today's fastest increasing issues into the world's greatest rebirth of entrepreneurship. Rather than focusing on humanitarian and altruistic approaches to refugee movement, we are focusing on the reawakening of human potential. We wish to return pride, dignity, and self-worth to individuals who have suffered as a result of societal injustices, war, and economic distress. We think that accomplishing our goal of 10 million individuals by 2022 is both attainable and ambitious.

We are very excited that you are interested in bringing the Hult Prize OnCampus Program to your campus! Being the face of social change and life-altering impact at your university is a huge responsibility - we couldn't be more thrilled with your decision.

Please feel free to take a few minutes to complete this early-bird application form so we can learn a little bit more about you. Please note the following:

- 2022/2023 Campus Directors interviews will happen on a rolling basis and will start on August 1st.
- Application answers should be in ENGLISH! Applications in other languages will not be considered.
- Apply before July 31st at 23:59 EST for a chance to win an entry ticket to the Hult Prize 2022 Global Finals to be hosted this September during the annual meeting of the Clinton Global Initiative in New York City. The raffle winner will be a selected Campus Director from the early-bird application pool of applicants and will be announced on August 15.

For any question, please email us at oncampus@hultprize.org

For details and application, visit: https://www.hultprize.org/

# Nugget 31: TECHNOVATION CHALLENGE FOR GIRLS

Code and UN Women are both great places to start if you want to acquire and practise the skills necessary to use technology to tackle real-world challenges. Girls all around the world have the option to participate in Technovation, which teaches them the skills they need to become leaders and entrepreneurs in the technology industry. Girls between the ages of 10 and 18 are taught how to recognize an issue in their community and develop a mobile app solution to address that problem. Following this, the girls are taught how to effectively convey their ideas and transform them into a fully operational business.

Ideation, Technology, Entrepreneurship, and Pitch are the four stages that students will go through as part of the Technovation curriculum, which is based on the concepts of design thinking and teaches them how to create a mobile app firm.

## Categories:

The issue that is remedied by your software ought to be classified under one of the following categories.

• Poverty

• Environment

• Peace

• Equality

• Education

• Health

**Benefits:** Applicants will get the knowledge necessary to successfully complete the following tasks throughout the course of the project:

- Conduct market research and financial analysis
- Carry out effective business planning
- Create an app prototype using MIT App Inventor

## Qualifications Required to Apply:

• The free online curriculum offered by Technovation is available to anybody who would like to use it.

• Technovation is looking for teams of female students from all around the world.

• The official Technovation competition is open to all female students up to the age of 18.

## How to Apply:

Interested applicants must apply online via given website.

For more information, visit http://www.technovationchallenge.org/get-started/

## Nugget 32: COMMON FUND FOR COMMODITIES GRANTS

The Common Fund for Commodities (CFC), which is located in the Netherlands, has issued a call for ideas in order to support initiatives for the development of commodities that are of benefit to the underprivileged in over one hundred nations all over the world. CFC is an organization that is based on membership, and it currently has 105 countries and 10 institutional members, including the European Union (EU), the African Union/African Economic Community (AU/AEC), the Common Market for Eastern and Southern Africa (COMESA), and, most recently, the Caribbean Community. CFC was established in 1975. (CARICOM).

The CFC seeks to support the implementation of innovative interventions that target new opportunities in commodity markets in order to facilitate commodity-based growth, the generation of employment, an increase in household incomes, a reduction in poverty, and an improvement in food security. This objective will be accomplished through the provision of financial assistance.

The intervention needs to be able to be scaled up, have a commercial viability, and be financially sustainable. Additionally, it should have a demonstrable and favourable influence on the players in commodities value chains.

The goals of the initiatives that are being funded by the CFC are as follows:

• On a social level, this should involve the generation of work opportunities, particularly for young people and women, the enhancement of household incomes, the reduction of poverty, and the improvement of food security.

• Economic: Increase output and productivity; strive for better local value addition; strengthen the competitiveness of producers, producer groups, and small and medium sized businesses; promote the growth of the financial sector.

• Establishing partnerships: Establishing productive and cost-efficient collaboration between producers, industry, governments, civil society groups, and other stakeholders for the sake of commodity-based development is a priority for the building partnerships initiative.

The CFC provides financial assistance to businesses and organizations who are active in supply chains for commodities.

The purpose of the CFC's financial support is to promote innovation as a means of encouraging established organizations and businesses to extend their core activities in ways that create additional opportunities for commodities and the stakeholders in the commodity value chains. This is accomplished through the promotion of innovation.

Partner organizations of the CFC may include cooperatives, producer groups, small and medium enterprises, processing and trading corporations, as well as local financial institutions. These organizations may also be bilateral or multi-lateral development institutions. The first application, which must be filed by organizations, is then followed by the review process, after which complete and thorough proposals can be presented.

Website: http://common-fund.org/

# Nugget 33: THE NESTLE PRIZE

The Nestlé Prize: The Nestlé Prize in Creating Shared Value will be awarded every other year to a person, a non-governmental organization (NGO), or a business for developing an outstanding innovation that:

• Has proven its worth on a small-scale.

• Has the potential to have a significant impact on a large-scale.

• Is designed to create shared value.

• Has a high promise of improving rural development, improving nutrition, improving access to clean water, or having a significant impact on water management and

• Is judged to be feasible and applicable on a larger scale or in other communities; and

• Is applicable on a larger scale or in other communities; and

The Nestle Prize in Creating Shared Value is an award that aims to stimulate and recognize innovative solutions to issues pertaining to nutrition, water, and rural development.

Nestle is of the opinion that developing nations should get a greater amount of investment in important social areas, and that recognizing really substantial and creative initiatives to address global issues is an effective way to generate shared benefit for all of us.

The winner of the Nestlé Prize in Creating Shared Value will be awarded an investment of up to 500,000 Swiss francs (CHF) over a certain amount of time. This investment is intended to support the further development of the invention and help bring it to a larger scale.

The Nestlé Prize is one of a kind since it requires the recipient to make a financial commitment that might extend over a number of years to assure the project's success.

The Nestle Prize in Creating Shared Value will recognize local efforts to practice the principle of Creating Shared Value and will be awarded to an individual, non-governmental organization (NGO), or business that has demonstrated innovative techniques for improving access to and management of water, improving the lives of farmers and rural communities, or delivering high nutritional value to populations suffering from nutritional deficits. Nestle will announce the winner of the prize in October of each year.

For more information, visit: http://www.nestle.com/csv/what-is-csv/nestleprize

# Nugget 34: AFRICAN DIASPORA MARKETPLACE (ICMPD)

2011 saw the opening of the second African Diaspora Marketplace, which was co-organized by the United States Agency for International Development (USAID) and Western Union (ADM II). ADM II promotes long-term economic growth and employment by assisting entrepreneurs of African descent and other backgrounds who are established in the United States by providing grant financing and other forms of financial and technical assistance. ADM II Awardees are individuals who have created or start-up enterprises in Africa that are both creative and high-impact, and who have demonstrated links to or experience in Africa. Each new commercial enterprise is eligible to earn matching partnership grants of up to $50,000 as well as several other types of technical support.

Follow this LINK:

**Contact:**

**Procurement and Grants Unit**

grants@icmpd.org

Gonzagagasse 1, 5th floor, 1010 Vienna, Austria

Tel: +43 1 504 46 77 - 2460

Fax: +43 1 504 46 77 23 75

## Nugget 35: WORLD PRESS PHOTO FOUNDATION MASTERCLASS WEST AFRICA

In order to choose participants for the World Press Photo Masterclass West Africa, the World Press Photo Foundation is seeking submissions from documentary photographers located in West Africa.

Accra, Ghana has been selected as the location for the Masterclass West Africa, which will help the most talented young visual journalists advance their careers. It is highly urged that any and all photographers who have worked on visual tales of daily life, environment, politics, and society submit an application for the Masterclass West Africa. The masters, who will be chosen to fit the learning requirements and preferences of the selected participants, will share their experience with the participants and give specific advice to each of the participants. The curriculum of the masterclass is organized around the participants' theme photo essays, which they are obliged to work on in preparation of the masterclass. The masterclass week features not only private training with each teacher, but also lectures given by that expert.

After previous editions in Mexico and Kenya, the Masterclass West

Africa is the third in the World Press Photo Foundation's series of satellite masterclasses. It is based on the formula of the annual Joop Swart Masterclass, which is run annually for the world's most talented emerging visual journalists. Previous editions of the Masterclass West Africa have taken place in Mexico and Kenya.

Those who are chosen to take part in the Masterclass West Africa are not have to pay any fees to do so, and the World Press Photo Foundation will pay for their transportation and hotel costs.

**Eligibility Criteria:**

Professional photographers with experience working on documentary photo stories who:

- ❖ Are nationals or permanent residents of the following countries: Benin, Burkina Faso, Cameroon, Central African Republic, Chad, Democratic Republic of the Congo, Gabon, The Gambia, Ghana, Guinea, Guinea-Bissau, Equatorial Guinea, Ivory Coast, Liberia, Mali, Mauritania, Niger, Nigeria, Republic of the Congo, Senegal, Sierra Leone, and Togo;
- ❖ Are under the age of 35; and
- ❖ Have a good understanding of English.

**How to Apply?**

- ❖ Interested applicants must submit their portfolio, biography with age and nationality, full contact details, as well as a short statement of their motivation in English describing what the masterclass might mean to their professional development.
- ❖ All required documents and information must be submitted via email.

For more information, please visit

https://www.worldpressphoto.org/

email communications@worldpressphoto.org or call +31(0)20 676 6096.

# Nugget 36: ENDEAVOR

Endeavor is a non-profit organization that was established in 1997 with the mission of promoting high-impact entrepreneurship. It does this by recognizing and supporting the continuous growth of a select number of entrepreneurs located in developing market nations (like in Africa).

The emphasis of Endeavor's investment strategy is to find and assist remarkable entrepreneurs operating in emerging markets. These entrepreneurs have the capacity to disrupt whole sectors, communities, and even countries. It selects people of all ages, ethnicities, and educational backgrounds, sending a meritocratic message to the developing world: that anyone, no matter where they live or what their background is, is capable of turning an entrepreneurial idea into a world-class venture through hard work, creativity, and values-driven leadership. Each year, Endeavor evaluates hundreds of prospective business owners and chooses to work with only those that have the potential to achieve extraordinary results. Candidates must first pass a series of local and regional interviews before presenting to panelists from its global business network at International Selection Panels, which are held four to five times each year. This is the first step in a rigorous, multi-step selection process that can last anywhere from 12 to 18 months.

Contact:

contact@endeavor.org

1 (212) 352-3200

Website: www.endeavor.org

# Nugget 37: ARGIDIUS-ANDE FINANCE CHALLENGE (AAFC)

The Argidius Foundation and the Aspen Network of Development Entrepreneurs (ANDE) have announced the Argidius-ANDE Finance Challenge (AAFC), which is a new competition designed to support innovative ways to provide capital to small businesses in emerging markets that require $20,000-$250,000 in early-stage capital. The Argidius Foundation is the sponsoring organization, and ANDE is the Aspen Network of Development Entrepreneurs. The purpose of the competition is to hasten the creation of creative and sustainable solutions in a variety of emerging markets, ideally with the intention of establishing models that can be duplicated by other businesses.

Follow this link to apply: https://www.aspeninstitute.org/

**Contact:**

The Aspen Institute

(202) 736-5800

**Location:**

The Aspen Institute, 2300 N St. NW, Suite 700 Washington, DC 20037

(202) 736-5800 (tel)

(202) 467-0790 (fax)

# Nugget 38: TONY ELUMELU ENTERPRENEURSHIP PROGRAM

Mr. Tony Elumelu, Chairman of UBA bank and Heirs Holdings, is responsible for the establishment of the $100 Million Tony Elumelu Foundation Entrepreneurship Program. It is an annual program with the goal of fostering entrepreneurship and providing opportunities for aspiring African businesspeople.

The program, which has a budget of one hundred million dollars and was unveiled at the offices of the Tony Elumelu Foundation in Lagos, Nigeria, will seek out and provide support for one thousand aspiring businesspeople from across the continent each year for the next ten years. A total of one million new jobs and an additional $10 billion in annual revenues will be added to Africa's economy as a direct result of the selection of 10,000 start-ups and young firms from across the continent.

The Tony Elumelu Foundation Entrepreneurship Program is available to those who are nationals or legal residents of any of Africa's 54 countries. Any for-profit business headquartered in Africa that has been operating for fewer than three years, including brand-new business ideas, is eligible to submit an application.

To apply, visit http://tonyelumelufoundation.org/programme/

# Nugget 39: AFRICA ENTERPRISE CHALLENGE FUND

The goal of the Africa Enterprise Challenge Fund (AECF) is to encourage private sector entrepreneurs in Africa by providing a fund with a capitalization of 207 million dollars that is funded by multilateral and bilateral donors. The governments of Australia, Denmark, the Netherlands, Sweden, and the United Kingdom, in addition to the International Fund for Agricultural Development, are among those that provide financial assistance to the AECF (IFAD).

Companies from the private sector are eligible to receive grants and grants that can be repaid from the Fund. These grants are intended to support innovative business ideas in the areas of agriculture, agribusiness, renewable energy, adaptation to climate change, and access to information and financial services. Competitions are the means by which the AECF makes its financing available. Companies operating in the private sector are encouraged to participate in AECF competitions by presenting their fresh and original business concepts with the purpose of winning AECF funding. The most promising concepts can win grants and loans without interest totaling up to $1.5 million.

**Contact Information:**

The Africa Enterprise Challenge Fund

10th Floor, ABC Towers, ABC Place

Waiyaki Way, Nairobi, Kenya

Tel: +254 20 269 9137/8/9

Email: info@aecfafrica.org

https://www.aecfafrica.org/

## Nugget 40: ROLEX AWARDS FOR ENTERPRISE

Since 1976, Rolex has been recognizing remarkable people who have the bravery and commitment to take on significant challenges by awarding them with one of their watches. Each Rolex Award for Enterprise is presented to a new or current initiative located anywhere in the world that merits funding due to its capacity to enhance lives or safeguard the natural and cultural heritage of the planet. The projects can be in any stage of development. By enhancing human understanding or conditions on the planet, these undertakings have had a profound impact on every facet of human existence.

Rolex Laureates come from a wide variety of countries and cultural backgrounds. They share a propensity for independent thought and the capacity to take on undertakings that need innovation and drive in the face of enormous odds. This is the common thread that binds them together.

**Focus Areas:** These grants provide financial assistance to pioneering projects in the fields of environmental protection, applied research and technology, or exploratory endeavours.

**Offered annually:** Yes

**Eligible Countries:** Any nationality

**Eligibility Criteria:** The Rolex Awards are open to anyone;

- over 18 years of age and under 30 years,
- of any nationality,
- Whose ground-breaking project is helping to expand the knowledge of our world and improve the quality of life on the planet.

The uniqueness, potential for effect, and feasibility of the projects, as well as, most importantly, the candidates' own spirit of business, are evaluated during the selection process.

**Prizes:** Each of the five winners will get 100,000 Swiss francs, which is twice as much as the amount of prizemoney that was previously presented to winners of the Youth Award. They will also receive a Rolex chronometer in addition to the benefits that come with worldwide recognition.

**Participation Instructions:** The application procedure consists of two stages: first, a pre-application, which can be submitted by any candidate who is eligible; then, a full application, which can only be filed by some individuals who have been invited to do so.

It is paramount to study the program webpage to check your eligibility details before applying.

For more details and application, visit:
http://www.rolexawards.com/about/apply

# Nugget 41: eVA FUND

The eVentures Africa Fund, also known as the eVA Fund, was established in January of 2010, and its primary mission is to pool financial resources and industry expertise from the Netherlands and Europe in order to make investments in internet-related businesses that are either small or medium in size in Africa.

eVA Fund is a venture capital firm that invests solely in early-stage businesses located in sub-Saharan Africa. MoboFree, Nomanini, Verviant, and Umuntu Media are just few of the companies in which it has invested.

The eVA Fund focuses on and exclusively invests in businesses that employ technology developed on the African continent to establish platforms of world-class quality that provide Africans with content created on the African continent. This comprises newly established companies in the following industries: internet and/or mobile applications, platforms, electronic commerce, and solution-providers (i.e. not in infrastructure and hardware).

**E-mail us:** info@eva-fund.com

**Follow us on Twitter:** @evafund

**Follow us on Linkedin:** www.linkedin.com/company/eventures-africa-

**Website:** www.eva-fund.com

# Nugget 42: SHELL LIVEWIRE NIGERIA

Shell LiveWIRE is a social investment programme with the objective of assisting young Nigerians in evaluating the possibility of launching their own company as a practical and workable avenue for pursuing a career. Young company owners and those with the potential to become business owners between the ages of 18 and 35 are offered assistance, access to training, coaching, and business mentoring through this programme.

The programme is mostly implemented in the Niger Delta region, and its primary objective is to motivate, inspire, and support young people between the ages of 18 and 35 to launch their own businesses through the supply of financial resources as well as training for young entrepreneurs.

The Shell Petroleum Development Company of Nigeria Limited sponsors the Youth Enterprise Development Program known as the Shell LiveWIRE Nigeria Program (SPDC).

**Contact:**

Shell LiveWIRE Nigeria

Sustainable Development and Community Development (SDCR)

The Shell Petroleum Development Company of Nigeria Limited,

Eastern Division,

P O Box 263 Port Harcourt,

Nigeria

Tel: +966 1 477 4402 +966 1 477 4402

E-Mail: info@livewire-nigeria.org

https://www.livewire.shell/

https://www.shell.com.ng/

# Nugget 43: AFRICAN WOMEN IN AGRICULTURAL R & D - (AWARD)

AWARD is an investment in the future of Africa through the expansion of the pool of talent represented by African women working in African research and development. At the core of the AWARD program is a fellowship that lasts for two years and assists African women in the sciences and other professional fields in advancing their careers more quickly.

The fellows are selected from all throughout sub-Saharan Africa, and they are given the opportunity to develop their scientific and leadership skills, and they are also partnered with senior scientists working in their respective fields who act as their mentors. AWARD is the result of a pilot fellowship program that G&D ran in conjunction with the Rockefeller Foundation, USAID, and the Syngenta Foundation for Sustainable Agriculture. This program was extremely successful and served as the basis for AWARD.

Email: awardfellows@cgiar.org

https://awardfellowships.org/

# Nugget 44: ASHDEN AWARDS FOR SUSTAINABLE ENERGY

The International Awards are intended for projects that are being carried out in less developed countries.

Winners of the award combat climate change and other environmental hazards, most notably deforestation, while also reducing poverty, improving people's health, welfare, and economic opportunities. These goals are accomplished through the use of locally generated, renewable energy.

There are a total of five international prizes, with the first prize in each category being worth £30,000 and the second place being worth $10,000.

A minimum of one of the following categories must be addressed for a scheme to be eligible for a prize:

1. Safety of food supplies

2. Health and general well-being

3. Illumination

4. Academics

5. Business Ventures

One of the five awards will take the form of a unique African Award, which will be presented to the most deserving initiative from that particular continent.

This award was established in recognition of the specific problems that climate change and poverty play in endangering the future of Africa, as well as the significant contribution that local renewable energy can make in addressing both of these issues.

Former awardees include the Kigali Institute of Science and Technology (Rwanda) for the use of biogas systems to improve sanitation and supply cooking fuel in large institutions, and the Mwanza Rural Housing Program (Tanzania) for the development of small businesses that produce high-quality bricks fired using agricultural waste. Both of these projects were completed in the region of East and Southern Africa (ESA).

Website: www.ashden.org

T: +44 (0) 20 7410 7023 E: info@ashden.org

The Peak, 3rd Floor 5 Wilton Road, London, SW1V 1AP

Registered in England and Wales as a company limited by guarantee.

Registered number: 05062574/ Charity number: 1104153

The University of Texas and Dell have collaborated to create the Dell
Social Innovation Competition, which is aimed at college students from
all over the world who are interested in applying their innovative ideas
to the alleviation of pressing societal issues. Dell's Social Innovation
program serves as a conduit for bringing students' solutions from the
conceptual stage into the real world.

The game of competition is an excellent way to hone your abilities in
the following areas:

Establishment of a project or business plan

presenting one's ideas to potential investors

Developing connections to available resources

You have the option of entering the competition with your proposal if
you are in possession of a ground-breaking concept or if you are able to
galvanize groups of people and resources in order to bring about broad-
reaching and scalable social change using your tenacity and personality.

It is possible for topics to include poverty alleviation and economic
development, human rights, peace and security, digital inclusion, global
health and AIDS, education, energy/environment/climate change, child

and youth development, volunteerism, food and potable water, microfinance, drugs and crime, elections and the government, as well as other topics.

The final prize consists of seed investment in the amount of $50,000 for the team or individual that comes up with the most inventive business idea to transform the world. This money can be used to launch or extend the project. Entries to the competition that concern the environment will be considered for a special reward worth $10,000 called the Tomberg Prize in Environmental Sustainability.

Each of the three teams that made it to the final round will automatically be given a space on the Global Giving website. This will provide them the opportunity to raise additional funding and get exposure to donors all over the world.

Website: http://www.dellchallenge.org/

# Nugget 46: WORLD SUMMIT YOUTH AWARD

World Summit Youth Award: The WSYA (World Summit Youth Award) selects and promotes best practice in e-Content and technological creativity, demonstrates young people's potential to create outstanding digital contents, and serves as a platform for people from all UN member states to work together in the efforts to reduce poverty and hunger, as well as to tackle ill health, gender inequality, lack of education, lack of access to clean water, and environmental degradation. In addition, the WSYA demonstrates young people's potential to create

Therefore, WSYA is both a platform for the world's young e-content creators, journalists and writers, application designers, and engineers, as well as a contribution to alleviating poverty, safeguarding the environment, sharing information, and empowering young people on a worldwide scale.

Through the networks of the World Summit Award (WSA), the UN Global Alliance for ICT, other participating UN Organizations and Agencies, governments and non-governmental organizations (NGOs), youth organizations, and anyone else who is dedicated to making a real difference in the accomplishment of the Sustainable Development Goals (SDGs), the WSYA is promoted in all of the UN member states.

**Application Eligibility Requirements for the Award:**

In order to be considered for the WSYA,

1. Individuals under the age of 30 must be the ones to conceptualize and carry out the initiative.

2. The product must be completely operational and functional at the time of the submission; projects that do not function properly will not be juried.

3. It needs to be able to be accessed over the internet (whether it is designed for fixed line, broadband or mobile use).

**The following requirements must be met for each entry:**

1. It must fall into one of the six categories: Fight against poverty, hunger, and disease; educate everyone; empower women; create your own culture; prioritize environmental sustainability; seek the truth; and

2. Any content that is found to be insulting, plagiarized, or otherwise in violation of human dignity or human rights will not be considered for evaluation.

3. To be carried out  by a person with the appropriate authority.

Website: www.youthaward.org

# Nugget 47: ONE Africa Award

ONE Africa Award: Innovators, civil society organizations, or advocacy groups based in Africa that have shown a commitment to and success in advancing one or more of the Sustainable Development Goals (SDGs) are encouraged to submit an application for the ONE Africa Award. ONE will select one winner for this award.

The purpose of this award is to acknowledge, promote, and recognize Africa-driven and Africa-led projects that are gradually bringing about positive change in individual lives, communities, and nations. The awardee will be recognized by ONE at an international conference that will take place in Africa in the month of November. Additionally, the awardee, along with the top four finalists, will be invited to share their success stories and lessons learned via The ONE Blog.

The purpose of the ONE Africa Award is to recognize, reward, and advance the exceptional work of an individual or civil society organization based in Africa that is dedicated to assisting Africa in achieving the Sustainable Development Goals (SDGs) on a local, national, or regional level. The award will be given to the recipient who best exemplifies these qualities.

The organization that is determined to be the most deserving of the ONE Africa Award will be granted a prize of up to one hundred thousand dollars as a way to recognize and support the recipient's exceptional contributions to the African civil society community.

**The following are the eligibility requirements for scholarship**

**applications:**

In order to be considered for the ONE Africa Award, persons and organizations must fall into one of the following categories:

Individuals or organizations from the African civil society that have shown a commitment to and been successful in assisting Africans in meeting one or more of the Millennium Development Goals are eligible for this award (SDGs).

Applicants may also include advocacy or pressure groups as well as think tanks that are engaged in governance activities such as the monitoring of resource flows and/or holding governments accountable to their Sustainable Development Goal commitments.

To apply, please visit: https://www.one.org/africa/the-one-africa-award/

# Nugget 48: SEEDSTARS AFRICA

Seedstars Africa is a member of the Seedstars Group, which is a venture builder based in Switzerland that is active and invests in more than 35 countries around the world, primarily in emerging markets in Asia, South America, the Middle East, and Africa. Seedstars Africa is based in Johannesburg, South Africa. SimplePay is a young Nigerian third-party payment processing firm that has produced a solution that has recently received an investment of 330 thousand dollars from Seedstars. This solution has the potential to disrupt payment services in Nigeria and Africa.

Visit www.seedstars.com  to apply

The foundation gives funding to non-profit groups that are working on unique projects and activities in one of three core areas of focus: health, nutrition, or environmental protection. Food grants will assist efforts to develop or increase access to food for consumption in Third World countries, as well as availability and safety of food.

Projects that promote sustainable agriculture; provide information and training to small-scale food producers and farmers; and control pests and diseases that damage crops that are important to developing countries are areas of interest.

It is the preference of the foundation to award grants for pilot projects and special programs that have the potential to be replicated; it is also the foundation's preference to support projects that employ and/or train personnel from developing countries; and it is the foundation's preference to support research concerning issues that are significant to developing countries.

Initiatives, particularly research projects, that are conducted in fields that typically receive insufficient funding will be given priority. Each year, grantees get a combined sum of $700.000 from the organization. The application process for the foundation consists of two stages: first, a concise idea paper is required, and then a select number of comprehensive proposals may be submitted.

At the stage of the concept paper, this system eliminates concepts that do not have a good chance of receiving the final funding. Requests for comprehensive ideas have a good likelihood of being granted. Send in two copies of a brief concept paper that follows the format of the application form for concept papers provided by the foundation.

The length of the idea paper should not exceed one typed page on both sides, and it should be accompanied by a preliminary budget that does not exceed one page.

The document outlining the proposal needs to be presented in English, and the information on the budget needs to be translated into US dollars.

Applications are not accepted by fax transmittal or via E-mail, unless prior approval has been given by foundation staff, address fuel and resource problems related to food production and preparation in developing countries; The geographic focus of the foundation is the developing world. Applicants must address fuel and resource problems related to food production and preparation in developing countries.

Organizations that are located in developing countries, as well as organizations that are located in rich nations but whose activities are of direct and immediate value to poor countries, will be given preference.

Website: http://cfhfoundation.grantsmanagement08.com/

# Nugget 50: ARMACAD

Unlike scholarships and fellowships awarded only to individuals according to their academic merit or financial need, the grants may be awarded to individuals and organizations. There are different types of grants, each with its unique set of guidelines, deadlines, and eligibility criteria. ARMACAD is actually the best tool that helps you find grants, fellowship and scholarships in various institutions around the world.

Also, grants are divided into different types according to their funding purpose: grants may be allocated for research purposes, fostering business activities, conducting human rights advocacy, preserving libraries, grants for ecological activities, grants for NGOs and foundations, etc.

For those individuals or institutions that search for funding, grants are the best option to consider because grants are an essential part of the academic activities of any research institute and these financial allocations are the main source to research in any field.

Each academic institution or laboratory, or other entity within the university strives to receive the best research grants. Grants are announced regularly by such organizations as World Bank, NED, UN, National Science Foundations in different countries, Government bodies, NASA, Space agencies, private foundations, big enterprises, museums, etc.

The main bulk of grants announced is grants for researchers, grants for research institutes and laboratories, grants for libraries, and grants for NGOs. US government grants and federal grants are announced every year and may continuously support research and scientific institutes.

Of course, there are also individual grants for researchers, grants for undergraduate students, graduate students, Ph.D. students, journalists, photographers, educators, etc.

Educational grants are a big part of grants given every year by the EU, Tempus, UN, USAID, and other international institutions. Another cluster of grants is assumed for small businesses. Small business grants are regularly announced again by government bodies and international organizations to foster small and medium enterprises worldwide. There are also many grants for women, grants for minorities, and travel grants for students and researchers.

https://armacad.info/opportunities/grants

# Nugget 51: WORLD BANK GRANTS

The World Bank makes grants to businesses and entrepreneurs all over the world. However, the majority of global grants are made in collaboration with governments. So, in order to access the world bank grants, you should be up to date on the latest world bank grants available to your country.

Civil society organizations, on the other hand, can continue to apply for World Bank funding.

As a representative of a civil society, you can always apply for the grant here

**HEADQUARTERS:**

THE WORLD BANK

1818 H Street, NW Washington, DC 20433 USA

Tel : (202) 473-1000

You can also contact their offices in Africa here

# Nugget 52: INTERNATIONAL MONETARY FUNDS (IMF) GRANTS

The International Monetary Fund (IMF) awards funding to nonprofit groups that aid the most vulnerable people in escaping social dependence, extreme poverty, and other harmful circumstances.

$10,000 is the average grant award.

In order to apply or learn more, click here

The AXA Research Fund's goal is to provide funding for exceptional researchers who are dedicated to addressing social issues around life and health, data and technology, the environment and economy, and economics. Grants from the AXA Research Fund are a creation of the AXA Foundation.

In 35 countries, including Nigeria, South Africa, and many other African nations, the organization had provided funds of up to €179 million for 563 research projects as of 2018.

Click here to read more about the grants offered by the AXA Research Fund.

# Nugget 54: THE ROCKEFELLER FOUNDATION GRANTS

Through grantmaking, The Rockefeller Foundations strives to advance human welfare on a global scale. Utilize our database to look up current and past grants by commitment and grant amount from the previous five years.

Please refer to the Foundation's 990-PF documents for a complete list of all individual grants as this database is updated on a regular basis.

To learn more about Rockefeller foundation grant click here

New York City, United States

The Rockefeller Foundation Global Headquarters

420 Fifth Avenue New York, NY 10018

A non-profit organization in the private sector, CIPE offers financial assistance in the form of grants to non-governmental business organizations around the globe, including chambers of commerce, employers' federations, trade associations, and private enterprise-oriented research teams. Without the involvement of the government, grants are given privately and directly to non-American corporate entities. The National Endowment for Democracy program's business representative was named by the US Congress in 1983 as CIPE. Every initiative undertaken by CIPE is open to the public and is funded by public resources. Commercial endeavors, trade and investment promotions, and partisan political action are not funded by CIPE.

Private enterprise and individual initiative are increasingly understood to be vital contributors to economic growth and human advancement around the world. The Center for International Private Enterprise (CIPE) works with other nations' private sectors to strengthen democracy and private enterprise as the cornerstones of economic growth and personal freedom.

To learn more or to apply for a CIPE grant click here

**NIGERIA**

Lagos

Tel: +234 1 029501659

Contact nigeria@cipe.org

**Washington, DC**

1211 Connecticut Avenue, NW, Suite 700

Washington, DC 20036

Tel: +1 202 721 9200

Fax: +1 202 280 1000

# Nugget 56: FORD FOUNDATION GRANTS

Since our founding 85 years ago, we have believed justice begins where inequality ends. The Ford Foundation provides funding to organizations that tackle the root causes of inequality and complement our global programmatic efforts. Our grant opportunities page lists the few programs or projects that are eligible for funding requests.

One of the most well-known philanthropic organizations in the world is The Ford Foundation. The foundations, which were founded in 1936, provide funding to groups throughout Asia, Africa, the Middle East, Latin America, and the United States.

Since its founding, the foundation has distributed nearly $16.3 billion in grants across the globe.

The Ford Foundation concentrates on programs that advance human knowledge, fight injustice and poverty, and promote democratic principles.

You can always write to the Ford Foundation and share your thoughts with them at any time.

To apply for a Ford Foundation grant or to learn more about the Ford Foundation grants click here

**CONTACT**

Ford Foundation

320 E 43rd St

New York, NY 10017

USA

Tel. (+1) 212-573-5000

The Next Titan is a Nigerian reality show for business owners with Heritage Bank serving as its primary sponsor. It offers a venue for businesspeople to connect, engage, and compare ideas. It is broadcast on Channels, TVC, and Silverbird. It is regarded as the best entrepreneurial reality show in Nigeria. The winner will ultimately receive $5 million and a brand-new automobile. The competition shows lasts for ten weeks, and before the final round, where the winner with the most creative idea is picked, the candidates are all put through a series of training sessions. Therefore, even when just one person receives financial assistance, everyone ends up winning because everyone else underwent a training procedure.

Click here for more information

# Nugget 58: BNI FOUNDATION

The only way to get a grant from the BNI Foundation is through a reference. In order to submit a grant application, a school or educational organization needs to have a connection with a Business Networking International Director, Chapter, Member, or Business Voices Team. In order to be considered for the award, applicants must be either schools or educational groups that align with our objective of assisting children and education. When it is deemed necessary, Givers Gain Grants will also be distributed to nonprofit organizations located outside of the United States.

The BNI Foundation is making a difference in the world by enhancing the conditions of children whose families are struggling financially, which in turn has a detrimental impact on the educational chances available to those youngsters. We back efforts that give teachers and non-profit groups access to resources that make it simpler for children to achieve their goals, either by removing obstacles in their path or by incentivizing them to pay attention in the classroom. For us, the most effective way to contribute to this transformation is to devote our time, treasure, and talent in various areas of education where we believe we can make a difference. Our Business Voices Initiative and our Givers Gain Grant Program are the vehicles through which we accomplish this goal.

Click here for more information on how to access grant from BNI
https://bnifoundation.org/programs/educational-grants/

TY Danjuma Foundation is a private, independent philanthropic organization based in Nigeria that is dedicated to enhancing the standard of living of Nigerians. It does this primarily through providing financial support to initiatives in the fields of health and education that are carried out in Nigeria by non-profit, non-governmental organizations (NGOs) that are registered in the country.

Lt. Gen. Theophilus Yakubu Danjuma, GCON, a retired Nigerian Army Chief of Staff and an adept and successful businessman, formed the Foundation in 2009. He was the driving force behind the organization's creation. The Foundation reached its full operational capacity in 2010 and has since continued to provide grants.

**The Foundation conducts its business based on the following fundamental principles:**

- Grant making that is both informed and responsive
- Participation in the community
- Participation of the government Accountability toward those who benefit
- Education and technological advancement
- Fostering a culture of charitable giving in Nigeria

In Nigeria, the TY Danjuma Foundation does the majority of its activities through non-governmental organizations and community-based organizations. Our strategy of working through partnerships is meant to build institutional capacity of groups, support innovation, and ensure that the funding provided meets the needs of the target beneficiaries and is culturally relevant. These goals will be accomplished by ensuring that the funding is culturally relevant. In doing so, the

Foundation encourages the recipients of its grants to strengthen the long-term viability of the projects they are working on by forming collaborations and partnerships with local, state, and national government entities.

The Foundation is also interested in working together with other organizations that award grants and international organizations that are active in its focus areas. When it comes to providing assistance for the activities of partners, the Foundation will, when necessary, seek for extra funds from other sources.

The dedication of the Foundation to documenting and analyzing the projects that it has funded is an important part of the work that it does. This helps the Foundation strengthen its future grantmaking efforts and contributes to the process of influencing policy and practice in the areas in which it is active.

A catalytic approach is taken by the Foundation in its grantmaking. We collaborate with our partners to better understand the difficulties that are encountered by the communities in which we operate in order to build solutions that can be put into action to answer the needs that have been identified. The mechanism through which we award funds is two-pronged; Both annual and discretionary grants are available.

To apply for the TYDANJUMA foundation grant click here
https://www.tydanjumafoundation.org/grantmaking

Grant for Individuals is an organization or a platform that connects people to other organizations, institutions, and government bodies that offer grant fundings, scholarships, and fellowships to individuals and organizations. These grant fundings, scholarships, and fellowships can be used for both personal and professional reasons.

In order to have access to grant opportunities, you will be required to sign up and or create an account on their platform. Foundation Grants to Individuals Online or https://grantstoindividuals.org

# Nugget 61: AFRICAN WOMEN INNOVATION AND ENTREPRENEURSHIP (AWIE)

A Special Consultative Status has been accorded to AWIEF by the United Nations Economic and Social Council. AWIEF is a pan-African women's economic empowerment organization that has won several awards (ECOSOC). The African Women in Enterprise Foundation (AWIEF) is dedicated to bridging the gender gap in business leadership and entrepreneurship across Africa.

AWIEF is an organization that has won awards for its work to empower women economically. Its mission is to assist women business owners in Africa in expanding their operations and realizing their full potential.

Our goal is to encourage the economic participation of women, as well as their growth and empowerment, by providing support for, and development of, entrepreneurial endeavours. Our dream is to see a prosperous and equitable Africa, one in which women-owned companies are given the tools they need to found and grow high-impact and long-lasting companies, which in turn contribute to an increase in Africa's gross domestic product and economic expansion.

Affirmative Finance Action for Women in Africa (AFAWA), an initiative of the African Development Bank (AfDB), and the African Women's Investment and Empowerment Forum (AWIEF) have joined forces to increase access to finance and markets for women-owned and women-led small and medium enterprises (WSMEs) in Southern, East, and West Africa.

The new AfDB-funded AWIEF program, titled "Solutions Catalyzing Increased Access to Capital for the Success of Women Entrepreneurs," has the overarching goal of boosting existing initiatives to combat gender inequality in order to foster inclusive economic development. More than 500 women- and minority-owned small and medium-sized enterprises (WSMEs) in eight African nations will get help for expansion, access to markets, and investment preparedness.

To apply for the 2022 entrepreneurship award click here
https://www.awieforum.org/

**ADDRESS:**

12 Bell Crescent, Dunrae Building

Westlake Business Park

Cape Town, ZA

**E-MAIL:** info@awieforum.org

**TEL:** +27 21 826 8878

**FOR GRANT WRITING SERVICES CONTACT TOYOSI GEORGE OBAYOMI ON 07032028335 OR** TOYOSIOBAYOMI@GMAIL.COM

QUESTCONSOLIDATORS@GMAIL.COM

# THE END

# ABOUT THE AUTHOR

## Toyosi George Obayomi

Toyosi George Obayomi is a cryptocurrency and blockchain enthusiast in addition to being an accountant, entrepreneur and a startup advisor.

www.ingramcontent.com/pod-product-compliance
Lightning Source LLC
Chambersburg PA
CBHW052111150726

48002CB00006B/2312